BIOGRAPHY OF A WARRIOR

PAINTED ON ANIMAL SKIN

CHEYENNE INDIANS OF THE PLAINS

(ORIGINAL IN CHICAGO NATURAL HISTORY MUSEUM)

FAMOUS INDIAN CHIEFS

By

JOHN W. MOYER

CHICAGO NATURAL HISTORY MUSEUM

Illustrated by

JAMES L. VLASATY

M. A. DONOHUE & CO.

CHICAGO · NEW YORK

COLORED ILLUSTRATIONS

CONTENTS

TO MY DAD

whose interest in the lives of

the American Indian aroused my curiosity

at a very early age,

this book is dedicated.

There are many books on the lives of famous Indians. Some are based on facts in recorded history, others are the results of a vivid imagination. To those of you whose interest is aroused by this book and who want more factual accounts of the so-called "red man," read the "Lives of Famous Indian Chiefs" by Norman B. Wood; "Handbook of American Indians" edited by Frederick W. Hodge, a publication of the Bureau of American Ethnology; "The Indian Tribes of North America" by Thomas L. McKenney and James Hall; and "Red Man's America" by Ruth M. Underhill.

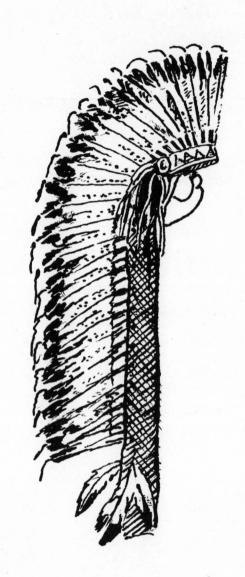

Red Jacket
1756-1830
Seneca

JAMES L. VLASA

CHAPTER I

Red Jacket

1756? — 1830

RED JACKET, the noted orator and Chief of the Seneca tribe, was born about 1756, probably at Canoga, New York. He was not of a ruling family and in earlier years was given the name Otetian, meaning "Always Ready." After being made a Chief of the tribe, his name was changed to Sagoyewatha, or in translation "the Keeper Awake."

His parents were both of the Seneca tribe, a part of the powerful League of the Iroquois, or the Six Nations of the East. He was of humble parentage and very little is known of his earlier years. Red Jacket was about twenty-nine years of age when history first recorded events in his life.

The Seneca eventually became the most important tribe in the League of the Iroquois. Other well-known tribes were the Mohawks and the Onondagas. The Seneca called themselves Tshoti-nonda-waga, meaning "people of the hills" which name probably referred to the small range of hills found near their homes.

The former range of this tribe was in western New York state between Seneca Lake and the Genessee River and earliest estimates give them at approximately 5,000 individuals. Today they are rep-

resented by several groups, each living in a different place and under various forms of Indian government. There are approximately 3,000 surviving members of the Senecas living on several reservations: the Tonawanda, Cattaraugus, Allegany, Onondaga and Tuscarora Reservations in New York; the Cornplanter Reservation in Pennsylvania and the Quapaw Reservation in Oklahoma. Also a few in Ontario, Canada living on the Grand River Reservation.

As a Chief of the Senecas, Red Jacket opposed his people going to war during the Revolution on either side. Many of the other Chiefs of the Six Nations, such as the famous Indian, Joseph Brandt, the great War-chief of the Mohawks, thought it to their best interests to join with the British. Although Red Jacket still would not give his consent to declare war, he took to the field of battle with his warriors after war was declared by the other Chiefs. Now his ability as a messenger and his outstanding intelligence and gift of oratory attracted the attention of the British officers. They knowing the Indians desire and weakness for unusual gifts, presented him with a beautiful, brilliant red jacket richly embroidered. Red Jacket took such a delight in this jacket that he was kept in such garments by the British all during the War and the jacket soon became a part of him. He wore it upon all important occasions and was known as Chief Red Jacket.

Red Jacket, like many other famous Indians who were known more for their oratory than for their fighting, was often accused of being a coward. He was a different Indian than the great War-chiefs, Geronimo and Tecumseh, who were best known by their acts of valour, but it is doubtful if Red Jacket was a coward. Red Jacket knew that the Indians would always lose out in a war no matter what side they fought on. He did not want his people to fight each other, nor to take part in the white man's battles. His oratory to both Indians and whites opposed war and no doubt because of this some reports brand him a coward.

At the close of the Revolution when many of the prophesies of Red Jacket became a reality, his influence among the Seneca was strengthened. It was now admitted by all, even his enemies, that the Indians fared much worse after the war was over than if they had taken no part in it. In 1784, the United States made a treaty with the Six Nations at Fort Stanwix, New York. This treaty provided for the cessation to the United States of western lands claimed by the Iroquois tribe. Red Jacket took a part in this council and it was here that he first met the great French General Lafayette, who had helped the cause of the Americans during the Revolution. Later, Red Jacket and the Senecas took part in the War of 1812, fighting on the side of the Americans against two other famous Chiefs, Tecumseh and his brother, the Prophet.

At the 1784 treaty council, Red Jacket, strange as it seems, did not favor peace with the whites. To him it meant only that what had happened in the past; a treaty that would take away not only the lands of the Indians but their way of life and freedom. After many days of talk on both sides, the treaty was finally signed and although now the Senecas were officially at peace with the United States, the tribes making up the Six Nations were dissatisfied with some of the terms of this treaty. Over the next six years, the Indians continued to commit war-like acts of violence until in June, 1791, President George Washington sent a delegation to the leading Chiefs asking them to visit him in the capitol at Philadelphia, the seat of Government at the time.

In the spring of 1792, fifty of the leading Chiefs of the Six Nations, including Red Jacket, called upon the President. It was during the conference between these Chiefs and the President that Washington presented to Red Jacket as a token of friendship, the silver Washington medal showing General Washington handing a peace-pipe to an Indian Chief. Red Jacket prized this medal highly and wore it and his famous red jacket on all state occasions.

Red Jacket was separated from his first wife and all his ten children died early in life of consumption, a bitter enemy of the Indians of that day. In later years he married again, the widow of a Chief whose name was Two Guns. This woman had several children and Red Jacket took them all into his home. All during his life, Red Jacket had opposed Christianity saying this was the religion of the white man and that the Indian had his own Gods. Later, after his second marriage, his wife and several others of the Senecas joined the church. This so enraged Red Jacket that he left home but in a few months returned as he missed his wife and children. He still though would not accept Christianity possibly due in part to the type of missionaries first sent to the tribes. He could see the wrongs being committed by the white man, not only upon the Indians, but upon themselves so could not understand how any new teachings could help the Indian. Near the close of his life, Red Jacket was formally deposed by twenty-six Chiefs of the tribe because of his opposition to

the new Christian religion. Some reports though say it was jealousy between these rival Chiefs that had more to do with removing Red Jacket from office than his opposition to Christianity.

Red Jacket, although now an old man, was not one to submit peacefully to such a disgrace. He worked upon the tribe through oratory and appealed to the Government officials until he was restored to his former position. Still, and until his death, he remained true to the religion of the Red Man and worshipped the Gods as he had been taught to do when a child.

Red Jacket visited the larger cities along the Atlantic coast many times in late years even as late as in 1829, a year before his death. It was on one of these earlier visits to Buffalo, New York that he again met Lafayette and they recalled their first meeting during the treaty of peace with the Six Nations at Fort Stanwix.

When Red Jacket was seventy-two years of age, he sat for the famous portrait showing him in his red jacket and the Washington medal around his neck. He had refused for many years to sit for a portrait but at length consented to do so after many had appealed to his vanity. At this time, although tall, erect and firm in bearing, many traces of hardship and dissipation show upon his face.

Red Jacket was suddenly taken ill of cholera in his seventy-fourth year. He lived for a few days, but on January 20, 1830, died in his home surrounded by his second wife and her children.

Even though he would never accept Christianity in life, he gave his wife full permission for a Christian burial a few days before his death. He asked to be buried among his own Seneca people. His wishes were carried out and he was given a simple funeral in the small mission church on the former reservation near Buffalo. Then in October, 1884, with the consent of the Seneca council, his body along with those of several other Chiefs was reinterred in Forest Lawn Cemetery, Buffalo, New York, and on June 22, 1891, a handsome memorial was unveiled at his grave. Another monument in memory of a famous Indian.

Black Hawk
1767-1838
Sauk and Fox

CHAPTER II

Black Hawk

1767 — 1838

BLACK HAWK was a Chief and distinguished warrior of the Sauk and Fox tribes. He was born in the Sauk Village at the mouth of the Rock River, Illinois, in 1767, and is best known as the leader of his people in the Black Hawk War of 1832. The Indian spelling of his name means in translation "black, or big bird," referring possibly to the crow or raven.

First written reports of the Sauk tribe is found in a journal of a Jesuit priest written in 1667. In this report he says these Indians were more savage than all other peoples he had met. If they or the Foxes found a person in the woods, they would kill him, especially so if that person was wearing a beard as these Indians hated the sight of the whiskers of a white man.

The Sauk and Fox Indians, two closely related Algonquian tribes, were also known as the Muskwaki Indians. These two tribes are the woodland people of our North American Indian tribes and were first reported on by the French in the second half of the 17th century. At that time they were living west of Lake Michigan in central Wisconsin. They were a restless and aggressive people and constant warfare

kept their numbers reduced so that at any given time the two tribes probably never numbered more than 3,000 individuals each.

In early years they were two separate tribes, the Sauks (or Sacs), "people of the yellow earth" and the Foxes, the "red earth people." In the early 1760's the Foxes were worsted in conflict with the French and joined up with the Sauk. From then on they were connected so closely with this tribe that the two have been long regarded as one tribe.

Later the Sauk and Fox moved from Wisconsin into Iowa where they found a haven from their enemies. This move though changed their woodland habits to those of the prairies, but being a people of much character they soon adapted themselves to these changes. Today we find the remnants of both tribes, now numbering a little over 1,000, on the Sac and Fox Reservations in Iowa and Oklahoma.

In later years, a tribe of the Sauks living near St. Louis, Missouri, entered into an agreement with the United States Government to relinquish all claim to their lands in Wisconsin, Illinois and Missouri. It is doubtful if the Chiefs of the tribe knew what they were doing, but after the treaty was signed, it was too late. When the other tribes found out what had been done, much bitterness and unrest came between them and the Foxes became so angry with the Sauk that the two tribes soon separated. Several agreements were entered into between the tribes before the treaty of 1804 was finally signed.

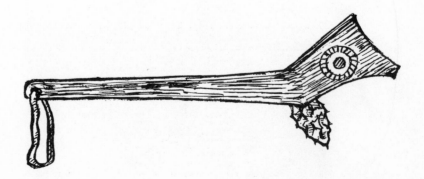

Out of this and the general unrest of all tribes of both Sauk and Fox, came the Black Hawk War of 1832. This War made the Indian Chief Black Hawk famous in the recorded history of our country.

Black Hawk's early life was spent mostly in war-fare. Great warriors and Chiefs, like all white leaders, learned from those that preceded them. Black Hawk fought under the famous Chief Tecumseh in the War of 1812 and must have gained knowledge in leadership and war-fare from this great Chieftain. Tecumseh had sought to form a confederation of all the neighboring tribes, to fight against the Americans in the War of 1812, but failed in this attempt.

When Black Hawk was only 15 years old, he distinguished himself in war, and at 17 led a war party against a nearby tribe of Osage Indians and won his first scalp. He continued these raids against the Osage, the Cherokee and others, and at 19 again led a war party against the Cherokee, but while victorious, his own father, who was the guardian of the tribal medicine, was killed. This saddened Black Hawk and for the next 5 years or so, he refrained from war and endeavored to acquire super-natural power to keep his hold over the tribe.

The treaty of 1804 surrendered all the lands of the Sauk and Fox on the east side of the Mississippi, but during the War of 1812, the Indians had been left undisturbed by the Government. Now settlers came into the territory and most of the tribes, led by the famous

Chief Keokuk, moved west across the Mississippi River into Iowa. Black Hawk, and a part of the tribe with those of the Winnebago, Potawatomi and Kickapoo he had enlisted in his cause, refused to move saying that when the treaty was signed they had been deceived by its terms.

Then in 1831, because of a series of killings and other acts of violence by the Indians against the settlers, Governor Reynolds of Illinois called on the Army for help. A conference was called by General Gaines in the hopes that a war could be averted, but Black Hawk would not listen to any terms. The soldiers were now ordered to march upon Black Hawk's village but a warning was given and he and his people escaped. The soldiers burned the village to the ground and General Gaines at once demanded the warriors come in for a peace talk, and on June 30, Black Hawk and his warriors signed the treaty agreeing to return to the west bank of the Mississippi to live.

Black Hawk, the wily Chief that he was, had no intention of abiding by this treaty. He tried in various ways to win other tribes to his side and to over-throw his own head Chief Keokuk, as it was his aim to bring war again to the whites and win back the original lands of the Indian.

In April, 1832, Black Hawk again recrossed the Mississippi at the head of about 2,000 people of his tribe of whom more than 500 were warriors. Again the army was called out and the settlers warned of

the danger of another war. Black Hawk continued up the Rock River expecting help from the Winnebago and Potawatomi, but only a few of these tribes joined with him. As the reinforcements Black Hawk expected failed and as the soldiers were nearing, he sent 3 Indians under a flag of truce to the soldiers' camp, but in the excitement and confusion among undisciplined troops, one of the bearers of the flag of truce was shot. This so enraged Black Hawk that he fell upon the soldiers with only 40 warriors, and in the suddenness and fury of the attack, all were driven from the field in a disgraceful rout.

Black Hawk now turned his Indians loose against the frontier settlements, burning buildings and killing their occupants. This war, although small in scale, sometimes ended in victory for the Indians, other times for the soldiers. In July, while he and the remainder of his band were trying to cross to the west side of the Wisconsin River, he was overtaken by the soldiers under General James D. Henry and defeated. With the remainder of his force, he retreated to the Mississippi and was about to cross when the steamer "Warrior" intercepted the Indians and shelled their camp. The following day the soldiers caught up with them and killed and captured nearly all. Black Hawk and one of his principal warriors, Neapope, escaped, however, to the north, but were later captured by the Winnebago and turned over to the Government.

After his capture, Black Hawk was sent east and confined for a

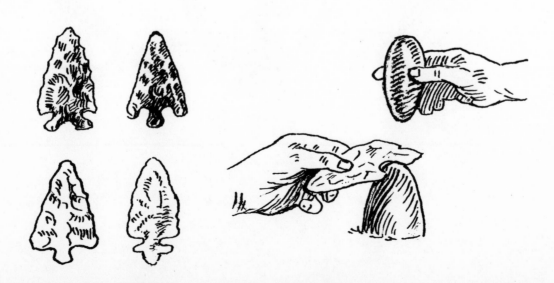

short time at Fortress Monroe, Virginia. He was later taken on a tour by the Government through many of the principal eastern cities. It was thought by the Government that a show of strength and what our cities were like would prevent him from planning any future uprisings. Black Hawk was much impressed by what he saw, as were the people he came into contact with, with him. In 1837, along with his former rival, Keokuk, he made a second trip through the east and later settled on the Des Moines River, near Iowaville. He died here on October 3, 1838.

Black Hawk was buried dressed in the military uniform and sword presented by General Jackson; a cane given him by Henry Clay; and medals from Jackson, John Quincy Adams and the City of Boston; this being the first of the white man's big cities he visited soon after his capture.

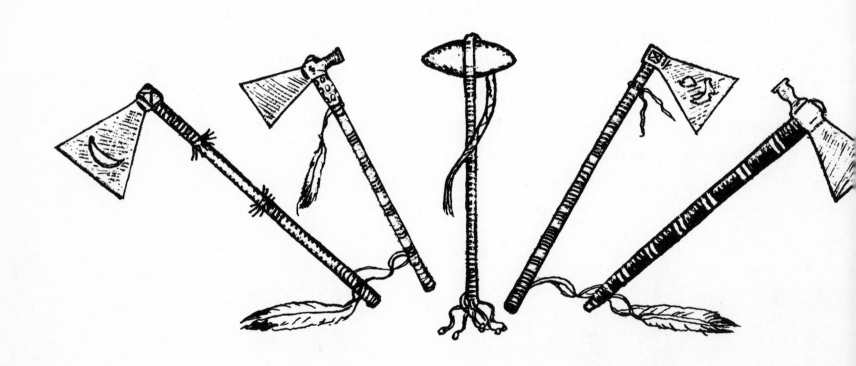

Tecumseh
1768-1813
Shawnee

JAMES E VLASATY

CHAPTER III

Tecumseh

1768? — 1813

A RENOWNED Chief and leader of the Shawnee tribe was Tecumseh. Born about 1768 along the Mad River near Piqua, Ohio, he was to become another famous Indian who took an active part in the early history of our country. The Indian name Tecumseh means "Shooting Star" in translation.

The Shawnee, an important tribe of Algonquian stock of North American Indians, were a restless people who liked to wander. They were thought to have migrated southward in very early times from their original home said to have been the territory north of the Great Lakes region. When discovered for the first time in the 17th century, the Shawnee were living in Tennessee and Kentucky. Toward the end of the 17th century the eastern division of the tribe moved north into Pennsylvania and early in the 18th century the other division began to drift north and west across the Ohio River. There about 1750 these two divisions united for the first time.

Of their early numbers very little is known. Some estimates give between 1,000 in 1736 to 2,000 in 1817. In 1910 the population of the Shawnee numbered 1,338. A part of the tribe lived for a short period

of time in Texas and Kansas, but today they are found living on the Quapaw and Shawnee Reservations, both in Oklahoma. They number a little over 1,000 persons.

At the time of Tecumseh's birth, the Shawnees were found living throughout the mid-western States. His early life was spent in Ohio and Indiana, although when a young warrior he visited many of the tribes living in the south. Early in his career, he tried to organize all Indian tribes from the Great Lakes region to the south into a confederation to halt the advance of the white settlers. While never able to do this, he did manage to band together the tribes of the Indiana Territory, but could never unite them into a great confederation of all the tribes.

Tecumseh was born into a ruling family, his father being a Chief of the Shawnee at the time of his birth. When only six years of age, his father was killed in battle and Tecumseh placed under the charge of an older brother, Cheeseekan. There were seven children in the family and soon another brother was also to become a famous figure in history. This brother was Tenskwatawa, or the Prophet. In later years, the Prophet both helped and hindered Tecumseh when he set himself up as a great medicine-man and councillor to the Indians. Tecumseh used his brother, the Prophet, in many ways when organizing the Chiefs of other tribes as the Prophet held a great deal of power over these Chiefs. Many were against the confederation as proposed by Tecumseh, but with the backing of the Prophet soon all were working for him in his efforts to keep the white man from taking over the lands of the Indians.

Cheeseekan, the brother of Tecumseh, gave him a great deal of care and attention during his early years. He taught him to hunt and the ways of Indian warfare and trained him well in oratory and leadership. In earlier years, Tecumseh showed a passion for fighting and many mimic combats and sham battles were fought among the children as this was their favorite sport. He soon became a recognized leader among his companions and when only sixteen years of age, took part in his first attack against the white settlers. It was after one of these earlier raids that Tecumseh first witnessed a common act of torture, practised by nearly all Indian tribes, the burning of a prisoner at the stake. He was so shocked and filled with horror that after he became a Chief, he would never allow a prisoner to be tortured by any of his people. Later in life, when he was in command of the Indians fighting on the side of the British in the War of 1812, he put a stop to the torture of prisoners by the British although it was the custom of all armies of the time to do this.

At about the age of nineteen, Tecumseh and his older brother, Cheeseekan, journeyed to the south. There they tried to enlist the Creeks, Cherokees and Seminoles into a confederacy to resist the advance of the whites and to stop the smaller tribes from signing away all their lands to the settlers. It was while in the south that Cheeseekan was killed while both he and Tecumseh were fighting with the Creeks. Now Tecumseh was chosen leader and although the youngest of the party, all were in favor of bestowing this honor upon him.

After an absence of nearly three years from his home in Ohio, Tecumseh returned in 1790. While he was away several battles between his people and the soldiers of the Army had taken place. Later, after his return home, he took part in the battle of Fallen Timbers and it was in this battle that another famous person in history, Mad

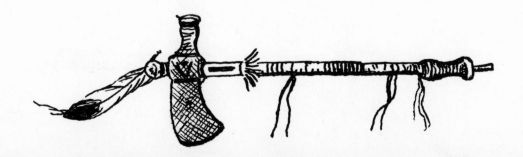

Anthony Wayne, crushed the Indians' power throughout the Ohio Valley. Later at the treaty council held at Greenville, Tecumseh could see that he would have to give up his plans for uniting the tribes. He settled along the White River in Indiana in 1798 and spent the next few years at peace and hunting the deer and other animals in the forests.

In 1805, many of the Shawnee, who were scattered and living among the different tribes, wished to again unite. Some of the lesser Chiefs sent a delegation to Tecumseh and he agreed to their proposals. It was at this time that his brother, the Prophet, became most powerful. The Prophet used his influence as a medicine-man to excite the Indians of his own tribe, the Shawnees, along with those of the Delawares, Wyandottes, Ottawas, Potawatomi, Chippewas, and Kickapoos. Later in 1808, the Potawatomi and Kickapoos gave the two brothers a tract of land along the Tippecanoe River in western Indiana for their people. A village was established known later as the Prophet's town and many Indians from all tribes now came here to live. Again Tecumseh thought of the confederation of tribes.

Not long after the building of the Prophet's town, Tecumseh left leaving his brother in charge and spent the next four years organizing all tribes from the Great Lakes to the south. He was not only a great and fearless leader and warrior, but one of the finest orators and statesmen of all Indians. Soon he had many tribes united for the purpose of holding the Ohio River as a permanent boundary between the white man and the Indian. In 1810, it was reported that Tecumseh controlled several thousand Indians of many different tribes, all united into a confederacy he had worked for so long and hard.

During Tecumseh's absence in the south, the Indians of the Prophet's town became so warlike that General Harrison, Governor of the Territory, determined to march upon the town to restore order. In September, 1811, troops came upon the town and as the Indians would not meet in council, on November 7, 1811, the battle of Tippecanoe took place. This battle was the turning point in the life of Tecumseh. After the battle which ended in victory for the troops, General Harrison burned the village to the ground and destroyed all its contents. This broke the power that Tecumseh held over the tribes as in losing the battle to the soldiers, all stores of ammunition, arms and provisions that Tecumseh had stored in the village were destroyed.

Tecumseh, whose confederacy seemed before the battle of Tippecanoe almost an accomplished fact, was on his way home when the fight took place. Returning to the village to see all in ruin and his years of work destroyed, as were the supplies and many of his people, was a great blow, more so as the battle had been fought in direct opposition to his orders.

Tecumseh had very little time to mourn his loss. A more important and bigger conflict now broke out the War of 1812. Because of such a humiliating defeat in the battle of Tippecanoe and as he could see his dreams and hopes of an Indian federation collapsing, he at once led his Indians to the support of the British. As he was now responsible for over 2,000 warriors under his leadership, he was made a brigadier-general in the British army, the first of two American Indians to hold such a high position, the other being General Ely S. Parker of the Civil War. Tecumseh took part in many decisive battles against the Americans while fighting with the British. He was a brave and

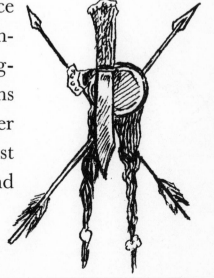

fearless warrior and often won the praise of soldiers of both sides for his valour.

After Commodore Perry's victory over the British on Lake Erie, Tecumseh covered the British General Proctor's retreat from Malden. During this retreat Tecumseh protested and asked the British to fight as he could see they were trying to escape leaving the Indians to do battle. Then on October 5, 1813, General Proctor was forced into the Battle of the Thames River, near Chatam, Ontario, Canada. In this, the bloodiest battle of the war, the British and Indians were defeated by General Harrison, Tecumseh's old foe of earlier days. It was also in this battle and on this date that Tecumseh was killed while in front of his Indians leading them in the fighting.

Before the battle, Tecumseh discarded his general's uniform and dressed himself in Indian deerskins. He gave his sword to one of the Chiefs fighting with him for safekeeping with instructions that it be given to his one and only son, as before the battle, he had had a premonition that he would be killed in the fighting. At the time of his death, he was in his forty-fifth year, one of the most extraordinary Indians of early times.

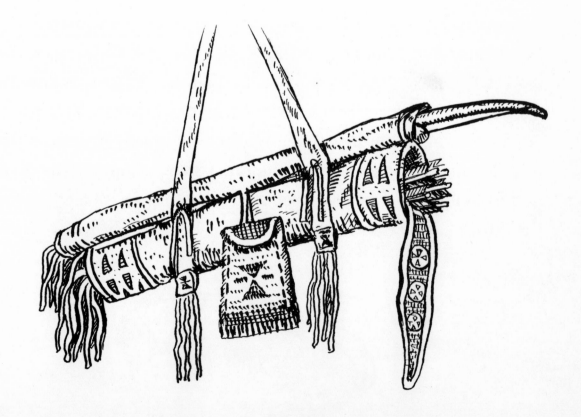

Yoholo-Micco
1790-1838
Creek

CHAPTER IV

Yoholo-Micco

1790? — 1838

ONE of the most noted Chiefs of the Creek nation was Yoholo-Micco. This famous Indian Chief was born along the Coosa River in Georgia about 1790, and died in Arkansas in 1838. His strange name Yoholo-Micco, in translation means, Yoholo, "Hallooer"; Micco, "Chief", such names being common among the Creek tribes.

As with so many Indians that played an important role in the early history of our country, very little is known of Yoholo-Micco's younger days. It is known that he was a brave warrior and one of the most persuasive orators of the Creek nation. He was the principal Chief of the Upper Creek tribe who were living in Tallapoosa County, Alabama, at the time of his birth.

The Creeks were the most important and powerful tribes of our southeast. They received their name from the British because of the many small streams running through their original territory.

The history of the Creek tribe begins with the appearance of DeSoto's army in their country in 1540. Before this date hardly anything is known of these Indians, but this is not strange as very little is known of the early history of the North American tribes.

In the early 18th century they were found occupying a large part of Georgia and Alabama and their population at that time was reported to be between 20,000-30,000 and divided into two groups, the Upper Creeks and the Lower Creeks.

The Creeks were hostile to the early Spanish explorers who came into their lands, but were nearly always friendly to the English settlers as they moved in. In later years and after many wars against the Americans, first during the Revolution and later the War of 1812, many of the tribe moved to the Indian Territory, now Oklahoma, where the remnants of this once numerous and powerful tribe now live. There are approximately 15,000-17,000 individuals officially recognized as Creeks living on and off the Five Civilized Tribes Agency in Oklahoma.

During early times, the Creeks were the leading tribe of the south. Being numerous in numbers and powerful in war, it was easy for them to resist the attacks of the northern tribes, such as the Iroquois, Shawnees and Cherokee, who tried time and time again to overpower them.

Into this powerful tribe, Yoholo-Micco was born. He, like all Creek men, was larger and more imposing looking than Indians of other tribes. He was about six feet in height, well formed, erect in carriage, and graceful in movement, and as a great and powerful orator, his outstanding appearance and voice always commanded attention in the treaty councils.

In 1813, a part of the Creek nation rebelled against the rule of the Government. Part of the tribe remained loyal and Yoholo-Micco led these warriors against the hostile Indians who were in rebellion. The Americans fighting in this war were under the command of General Andrew Jackson, and it was while fighting under Jackson

that Yoholo-Micco gained fame as a leader of his people. The war ended in 1814 in complete defeat for the hostile Creeks and in the treaty council that followed, a greater part of their lands was ceded to the United States.

Yoholo-Micco was a good family man and the father of several children who were given every advantage of an education that the country afforded. His sons were taught the civilized ways of the white man, and his daughters married well into the tribe.

Yoholo-Micco was mild in manner, with a sincere and generous disposition. As he always favored the white man's way of life and took so decided a part in favor of the plans to improve the conditions of his people, as prepared by the Government, he soon became unpopular. This caused him, in later years, to lose his place and influence in the general council of the tribes when another was appointed to take his place as their leader.

Before Yoholo-Micco was deposed as Chief, which later led to his death at an early age, he was the principal signer of various treaties. As with all such treaties between the Government of the white man and the different Indian tribes throughout the country, these treaties called for ceding Creek lands and eventually agreeing to emigrate beyond the Mississippi to new homes.

The Creek nation, both the Upper Creeks, of which Yoholo-Micca was Chief, and the Lower Creeks, whose chief was Opothle-Yoholo were ruled over by Little Prince, an aged Creek Chief. At this time, the Government was trying to get the Creeks to move peacefully across the Mississippi as their lands were gradually being taken over by the settlers. The Creeks were divided on this question and after many councils, all of which ended in failure by the Government to

get the tribes to come to terms, it was requested that a deputation of all the leading Chiefs of the Creek nation visit Washington.

In November, 1825, thirteen of the leading Chiefs of the Creeks, journeyed to Washington. They remained at the capital several weeks making quite an impression on the residents there as they went about in their strange and colorful dress. In January, 1826, a new treaty was drafted by which the Creeks surrendered all their lands in Georgia and this was agreed to and signed by the Chiefs.

Yoholo-Micco was one of the Chiefs sent to Washington and the newspapers there referred to him as "the favorite orator of the Creek nation," as it was Yoholo-Micco who did most of the talking for the Indians. Yoholo-Micco took along on this trip his son, Mistippee. Mistippee was a remarkably handsome boy and his father gave him all the advantages in regards to an education. It was no doubt for this reason that he was allowed to accompany his father on this journey to the white man's capital city.

Even though the Chiefs of the Creek nation had agreed by the treaty signed in Washington in 1826 to move to new lands beyond the Mississippi, it took many years for this to become a reality. Now Yoholo-Micco was in disgrace and his place had been taken by another of the tribe. In 1838 most of the tribe had begun the move westward and Yoholo-Micco consented to go, but because of the hardships of the journey and no doubt because his spirit had been broken when wrested from his position by his own people, he died in Arkansas while on way to his new home. He was only 48 years of age at the time.

Osceola
1803-1838
Seminole

CHAPTER V

Osceola

1803 — 1838

THE MOST famous and best known Chief of the Seminole Indian Tribe was Osceola. He was born on the Tallapoosa River, Georgia, in 1803. His name in translation means "Rising Sun." Osceola later in life sometimes used the name of Powell, as his mother married a white man by the name of William Powell after the death of his father.

The Seminole were an important tribe of Muskhogeon stock of American Indians. The name Seminole was originally given to the Creeks and Hitchitis living along the lower Chattahoochee River and who later separated and migrated to the central and southern peninsula of Florida about 1775 following the destruction of the Creek and other tribes of the original territory. The name Seminole means "Runaway."

This separation from the main body of the Creeks and Hitchitis was due chiefly to over-population of the older villages by undesirable persons in the form of criminals driven out of their home territories. Another cause of this separation was the encroachment by white settlers onto their lands making it impossible to live the free and easy

way of life they enjoyed. Florida, at this time, was wild and unsettled and much of it swamps and jungles which were ideally suited as a place to start a new life for a people such as the Seminole.

No early estimates of their numbers are given as many are of mixed and negro blood. On their final surrender, after two wars and numerous conflicts with the Government, about 3,800 were moved to the West where they now form one of the five civilized tribes resident on reservations. Others of these tribes are the Cherokees, Choctaws, Chickasaws and Creeks. The Seminoles possibly number under 1,000 persons including some negros and adopted whites, a few living in Oklahoma, but most are found on the Seminole Agency and Reservation in the southern part of Florida living as near primitive conditions as it is possible for one to live today. They are a colorful people, but reserved and difficult to know.

The Seminoles in early years became involved in several wars with the United States; first in 1812, and later in 1817. This last war was known as the first Seminole war, but it was the war of 1855 that is recorded in history as the Seminole War.

In 1823 the Seminoles ceded all of their lands except a part known as the central reservation to the United States Government. This 1823 treaty provided they move to a new reservation west of the

Mississippi, the Indian Territory in Oklahoma, but the treaty was bitterly resented by a large part of the tribe who refused to abide by the terms and prepared to resist. It was about this time that Osceola was chosen leader of those Indians who opposed the treaty and at once he led them in open revolt.

At a very early age Osceola was left fatherless and alone with his mother to guide him in the ways of the tribe. When about fifteen, he joined a band of hostile Creek Indians and fought against the United States. Later, when peace was established, he emigrated to Florida with the remaining members of the Creek tribe and joined with the Seminoles.

Osceola as a young man was noted for his athletic prowess and was skilled in the sports of ball playing, running and wrestling. His physique was described as tall, slender and straight. He had a pleasant countenance, which at times took on a melancholy look; was light of skin, and had the appearance of a half-breed as his paternal grandfather was a Scotchman, who had married a Creek woman.

After moving to Florida, Osceola became well known to the officers of Fort King, visiting the Fort frequently and performing many services for the Army. His standing with the officers gave him greater prestige among his own people which was what he needed,

as his position in the tribe was lower than others and as he could not become a Chief by descent, he had to win the approval of the leaders of the tribe by other means. Later, when he sided in with those of the tribe that opposed the treaty which would move them from Florida, he became Chief of this band and later became well known during a Seminole uprising of 1835.

About this time Osceola's wife, the daughter of a fugitive slave, was seized by the whites and carried off into slavery. This, more than anything else hastened his desire for battle and revenge. The Seminoles began the war by burning, killing, and destroying settlers' property, many times against settlers who were their former friends. Several important people were killed at the beginning of the war, including the principal signer of the treaty for their removal from Florida.

Now under the able leadership of Osceola, the Indians raised havoc with the United States troops as they were accustomed to a life in the swamps and jungles of central and southern Florida where the troops could not follow. Osceola first took the women, children and older people of the tribe deep in the swamp and hid them so they would not be found by the troops. In this way, he relieved his warriors of the worry of their families and they were free to fight. The

Army sent in troops under several different commands, but due to the nature of the country and the difficulty of travel and communications, they could not bring Osceola and his band to battle. Time after time, the troops became bogged down in the swamps and had to fight their way out. Osceola continued to harass the soldiers and the command of the troops was changed again and again in hopes that some new leader would be able to bring the war to an end.

As the war had now lasted several years, the public clamored for a settlement. General Jesup, then in command and maddened by the public's demand for action and an end to hostilities, seized Osceola and his leaders while holding a conference under a flag of truce; another black page in American history in the Government's many such shameful acts against the American Indian. This seizure of Osceola brought about the end of the war.

The Seminole War lasted for nearly eight years ending in August, 1842. It took the lives of nearly 1,500 American troops and civilians and cost the Government over $20,000,000. As with all such wars, the Indians lost as the Seminoles were now faced with expatriation from Florida. This, like all Indian wars of the past, followed a pattern. There were acts of vengeance by both settlers and Indians. While the Seminoles were not numerous, they were scattered through-

out the swamps in an area the troops and those whites fighting with them could not penetrate, all of which prolonged the war and caused such a tremendous loss of life and property.

Osceola, after his capture, was first imprisoned at St. Augustine and later in the dungeon at Fort Moultrie, South Carolina. Now his spirit broken, brooding over the manner in which he had been betrayed and loss of freedom, soon brought on his death. He died in prison at Fort Moultrie January 30, 1838 at the early age of 35 years. Reports tell us that when he realized death was near, he requested that he be allowed to dress in the clothes that he wore while leading the Seminoles into battle.

Red Cloud
1822-1909
Sioux

JAMES L. VLASATY

CHAPTER VI

Red Cloud

1822 — 1909

ONE OF THE last great War-Chiefs of all Indian tribes was Red Cloud of the great Sioux nation. He was born at the forks of the Platte River, Nebraska in 1822. In earlier years and as a young man he was referred to among his people as "Scarlet Cloud," but later known as 'Makhpia-sha' or Red Cloud. The name is said to refer to the scarlet blanketed warriors of the Sioux as they covered a hillside like a red cloud grouped for battle.

Red Cloud did not come from a ruling family. He became a Chief by virtue of his forceful character and deeds. As a member of the Snake clan and, because of his many outstanding virtues he became a principal Chief of the Oglala Teton Sioux, the largest band in the Sioux nation. He was probably the most famous and powerful Chief in the history of the tribe.

The Sioux tribe of North American Indians were a part of the powerful Siouan speaking family of tribal peoples. The largest and most numerous of these Siouan families were the Sioux, or Dakota Indians. Their original territory was that west of the Mississippi River and in early years they numbered about 15,000 individuals.

The Teton Sioux, possibly the tribe best known to us today, embraced several sub-tribes among which are the Blackfeet, Oglala and the Hunkpapa. There are a few others but these are the ones known today as belonging to the Sioux tribe. The descendants of this powerful and numerous people still are found in large numbers, possibly 20,000 persons, living on several reservations. These are the Fort Peck Agency and Reservation in Montana; the Standing Rock Agency and Reservation and the Fort Tohen Reservation in North Dakota and the Cheyenne River Agency and Reservation, the Pine Ridge Agency and Reservation and the Rosebud Agency in South Dakota.

The Teton-Dakota Sioux were formerly made up of bands of Indians living west of the Missouri River. They were often referred to as "people of the plains." Other famous Chiefs of these same people were Sitting Bull and Crazy Horse. The Sioux were courageous warriors, daring horsemen and skillful hunters. They were well trained in the characteristics of the early fighting Indian; bravery, cunning, treachery, hospitality and each warrior true to all other warriors in the band.

Red Cloud became a bitter enemy of the white man because of the white man's disregard of the Indian and his way of life. He could see nothing but disaster for his people and the destruction of their hunting grounds if settlers were allowed access to these lands. Red Cloud's father died of drink which was introduced into the tribe by

early traders and he could see the harm to their peaceful ways of life if things like this continued.

In 1865, the Government undertook to build a road to the gold fields of Montana through lands where the Sioux hunted buffalo. Red Cloud could see the end to their main source for food and clothing if this was allowed and he at once headed the opposition to the Government for his tribe. At the beginning only a small detachment of troops was sent out to begin operations on the road. These were easily captured by the Indians and held prisoner, but after a short time were released. As the Government did not want this sort of thing repeated a peace council was called in June, 1866 at Fort Laramie, Wyoming to see what could be worked out. This council was attended by Red Cloud and the other principal Chiefs of the Sioux but while the council was in progress a company of troops under the command of Colonel Henry Carrington rode in. They had orders to build a string of forts deep in the territory hunted over by the Indians, and to open a trail to Montana. When Red Cloud heard of this it made him distrust the whites more than ever and he refused to remain in council. He could see that it would be useless to talk of peace with the soldiers ready to carry out their orders, so he and all the other Chiefs left the council in anger.

Colonel Carrington now set about on his mission; first, to build Fort Phil Kearney along Piney Creek near the Big Horn Mountains and later to open the Bozeman Trail to Montana. When Red Cloud

was advised that construction on Fort Kearney had begun he at once gathered his warriers and harassed the soldiers day and night in trying to stop their work. This made conditions very difficult as Red Cloud with over 2,000 warriors under his command, all as determined as he that the Fort would not be built, were ready and eager for battle. In December, 1866 after months of hardship and suffering by the troops as they tried to build the Fort and to carry out their orders, a serious blow was dealt by the Indians. A detachment of 81 men sent out to cut logs was surrounded by Red Cloud and his warriors and every man killed and scalped. After this it was thought by those in command that the Fort should be abandoned, but the Government was determined to continue with its plans.

Month after month this type of fighting continued while the work was in progress. Then in August, 1867 another similar engagement took place when the detail for cutting wood left the Fort. But this time the soldiers were on the look-out for the Indians and they were also equipped with the new rapid-fire rifles just brought out by the Government. In this encounter the detail was rescued by a relief column sent from the Fort, but just in time as it was 32 men against several thousand Sioux.

Conditions still remained serious as the Indians kept the soldiers confined to the Fort making it impossible to get fresh water and game for food without also sending out an armed escort. Not a single wagon train had been able to move over the Bozeman Trail the Government

was trying so hard to open. In April, 1868 an investigation was ordered by the Government to see what was delaying construction of the forts and later a council was called with the Indians at Fort Laramie to see if a treaty could be worked out. Again Red Cloud repeated his demands made at the 1866 council: namely that all plans for the building of forts in Sioux territory be abandoned and the Bozeman Trail closed for all time. After some deliberation the Government could see that it would be useless to try and get the Indians to agree to the present plans for developing the West and a treaty was finally drawn up agreeing to all the Indians' demands. Red Cloud refused to sign this new treaty until the Fort was actually abandoned and as there was no other recourse the Government had to agree, or the Indians would continue to fight.

In August, Fort Phil Kearney was evacuated and the soldiers were still within sight of the Fort when the Indians applied the torch burning the buildings to the ground. The land of the Sioux was finally free of the invaders for the time being. Red Cloud put his signature to the treaty at Fort Laramie November 6, 1868 ending one of the few wars when the Indians won out over the Government.

After signing this treaty Red Cloud never again took to the warpath. He had won one victory for his people and he knew he could not win another. He took no active part in the Sioux uprising of 1876 led by the famous Sioux medicine-man Sitting Bull, nor did he support the outbreak of 1890-91, the Messiah Craze, or Ghost Dance.

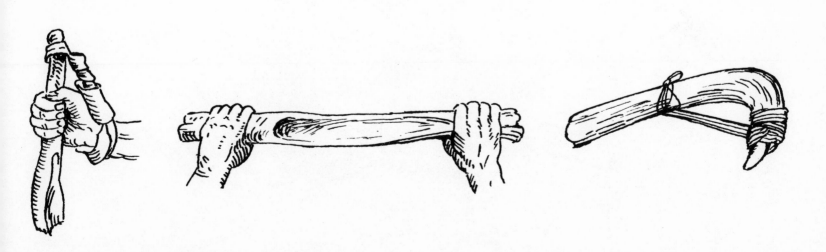

Later after gold was discovered in the Black Hills he became convinced of the hopelessness of attempting to hold to the territory and reluctantly joined in the agreement of cession of 1876.

As a warrior and War-Chief, Red Cloud ranked first among the people of his tribe. He was brave in battle, outstanding as a statesman and courteous in all council proceedings. He was a patriot from the Indians' standpoint and because of his high position in the tribe was a delegate to the capital in Washington upon several occasions.

Red Cloud became partially blind and very feeble in his later years. He made his home on the Pine Ridge Reservation in South Dakota in a house built for him by the Government and died there on December 10, 1909.

Dull Knife
1828(?)-1879
Cheyenne

JAMES L. VLASATY

CHAPTER VII

Dull Knife

1828(?) – 1879

DULL KNIFE was one of the War Chiefs of the Cheyenne tribe. Very little is known of the personal life of this famous Indian, but it is believed he was born about 1828, possibly in the State of Colorado. His Indian name first appeared on a treaty signed at Fort Laramie, Wyoming, as "Tah-me-la-pash-me" or Dull Knife.

The Cheyenne were another important tribe of Algonquian stock. In the 18th century they lived along the Cheyenne River in eastern North Dakota, but were later driven southwest by the powerful Sioux to the forks of the Big Cheyenne, near the Black Hills where the Lewis and Clark Expedition found them.

They were originally an agricultural people, but with the advent of horses they turned, like other tribes of the Plains Indians, into nomads. At this early date they numbered a little over 3,000 individuals.

The Cheyenne, like all other Indian tribes of early days, committed the usual atrocities upon the settlers who took over their home lands, but these acts were always in retaliation for such as the Indians realized they could not exist if their hunting grounds were destroyed. In 1865 the chiefs of the tribe consented to go on a reservation.

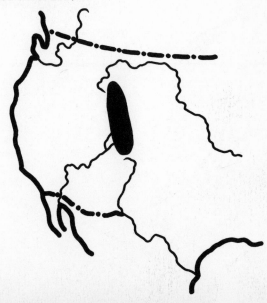

Today the Northern Cheyenne are on the Northern Cheyenne Agency and Reservation, Tongue River, Montana while the Southern Cheyenne are found on the large Cheyenne and Arapaho Reservation in Oklahoma. They number about 4,000 persons on these two reservations.

In early years, the Cheyennes were divided into two groups, the Southern Cheyenne and the Northern Cheyenne. Dull Knife was a War Chief of a band belonging to the Northern group. The modern history of this tribe begins with the Lewis and Clark expedition in 1804.

About this time the Cheyennes were being forced more and more into the plains by the mighty Sioux, and here they established camps along the upper branches of the Platte River in Colorado. In 1851, by the treaty of Fort Laramie, the separation of the tribe became final and the Southern Cheyenne moved into Arkansas and the Northern Cheyenne into Colorado and Nebraska.

The Cheyenne in early days were not war-like in their contacts with the white settlers. It was only after the settlers began to take over their lands, to slaughter and drive off the buffalo, combined with the sufferings and mistreatment by both settlers and Government, did they turn aggressor.

Into this tribe, called by some "the Fighting Cheyennes," Dull Knife was born and upon attaining manhood was made a War-Chief of the tribe. Not only did he lead his people in raids and battle against Indians of hostile tribes and the settlers, but in the treaty council that always followed a battle, Dull Knife was always present to represent his people.

Dull Knife, although a good man and a brave warrior, was not an organizer or orator and was noted most for taking over after others

had planned the strategy of battle. Even though he was not the organizer and famous for his speeches like some of the Chiefs of other tribes, he was always a leading figure because of his bravery.

Dull Knife belonged to a group of Chiefs of the Cheyenne that numbered among them Little Wolf, Wild Hog and the famous fighting Chief, Roman Nose. These War-Chiefs were the leaders of the different fighting bands within the tribe and led these groups in all kinds of duties besides fighting. Among the Cheyenne, the War-Chiefs were chosen to hold office for ten years. At the end of this period they could be re-elected for another term, or were allowed to name one to succeed them—sometimes a son to take their place. Before Dull Knife's death, he had named his son, Bull Hump, to succeed him, but when this time arrived, Bull Hump declined on the grounds that Chiefs were now no longer needed. This was in 1883.

Down through the years the Cheyenne had been fighting desperately to keep their lands and way of life, but were gradually being forced into a treaty along with another tribe, the Arapaho. Soon this treaty, like many others, was broken by acts committed against the Indians by both the Government and settlers and the Cheyenne went on the war-path again. In 1876, the Northern Cheyenne, which included Dull Knife's band, joined with the Sioux under Sitting Bull and took a decisive part in the Custer massacre, on the Little Bighorn, Montana Territory in June, 1876.

After this victory, the tribes separated and Dull Knife led his band into winter camp, but on November 25, 1876, cavalry troops under Colonel Mackenzie found their camp and attacked at daybreak, destroying all the lodges and capturing the Indians' horses. Although many of the Cheyenne were killed, others escaped but because it was

now winter and their homes, horses and food destroyed, they soon surrendered. Dull Knife and the remnants of the tribe were now moved to the Indian Territory in Oklahoma.

A few months in their new homes saw these people sick with a disease new to them, malaria. Many officials now agreed that they should be moved back to the high plains of the north to combat this disease, but no effort was made by the Government to do so. Finally the Indians openly announced their intention to go north, and the march was begun in the fall and winter of 1878.

These few Cheyenne in their last desperate attempt to return to their former homes were led by three War-Chiefs, Wild Hog, Little Wolf, and Dull Knife. There were 89 men and 146 women and children in the band. As soon as their plan became known, troops numbering several thousand were sent to bring them back. The way of the Indians was over open country where there was no opportunity to avoid the soldiers or to hide, and little chance for rest, or to get enough food by hunting. As the Indians were so far outnumbered they tried to resist fighting in order not only to save their warriors, but their women and children too, but on the night of January 9th, 1879, the troops caught up with them and most of the warriors, including Dull Knife, were killed. A few of the Cheyenne under Little Wolf made good their escape, but were captured and later what few remained were assigned to the reservation in Montana, along with the remnants of the Northern Cheyenne tribe.

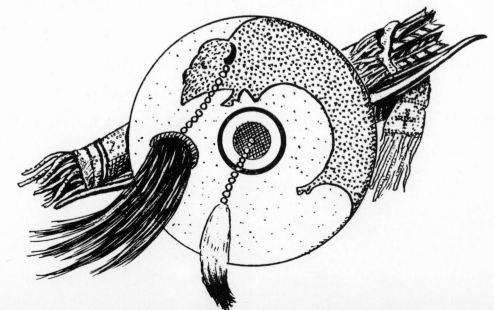

Sitting Bull
1834-1890
Sioux

JAMES L. VLASATY

CHAPTER VIII

Sitting Bull

1834 — 1890

ONE winter's day in 1834 along the Grand River in South Dakota, there was born into the Hunkpapa tribe of the great Sioux nation, an Indian boy. This Indian boy was to grow up to become one of the most famous Indians in American history. His name was Sitting Bull, shortened from "Sitting Buffalo Bull."

Sitting Bull's father was a subchief of the tribe and often let the young boy accompany him on the hunt and on the warpath. At 10 years of age, he was a hunter of the buffalo and at 14 he was allowed to go on the warpath with his father against the Crow. In early years and on into manhood, Sitting Bull saw the lands which had always been the home of his people gradually being taken over by the white man. This made him hate the whites more and more causing him to spend his entire life in warfare against the United States Government.

Sitting Bull became a medicine man rather than a Chief. His power over the Sioux was great and he alone is blamed for the Custer massacre. He was not a great warrior in battle, but more of an agitator who kept the Indians constantly stirred up over the white settlers who were moving into and taking over their hunting grounds.

In 1875, Sitting Bull and two other Sioux Chiefs visited Washington. There they were granted an audience by President Grant, who was anxious for a treaty to be signed which would bring peace between the Indians and the whites. As this treaty, like all others previous, would take away the hunting grounds of the Sioux and confine them to Government reservations, the Chiefs would not sign.

Later in 1876, after the failure of the Government to come to terms with the Indians, a campaign was organized against Sitting Bull and others of the Sioux tribe. This brought about the famous battle of the Little Big Horn River in which General George A. Custer and his entire Seventh Cavalry were massacred.

When gold was discovered in the Black Hills, thousands of men disregarding the warnings of the authorities to keep away from the territory claimed by the Sioux, came to search for this precious metal. The Indians in retaliation began stealing, burning and killing throughout Montana and Wyoming. Wagon trains taking settlers to new homes in the west and isolated farms were attacked and all occupants captured or killed. The army now moved in and drove Sitting Bull and several thousand of his warriors into the Big Horn mountains. General Custer was sent to locate the camp of the Sioux and came upon them early in the morning of June 25, 1876. Without waiting for reinforcements, Custer at once ordered the attack, but as the Indians had laid a trap, all, including Custer, were killed. Several accounts of the fight say there were only two survivors, an Indian scout named Curley of the Crow nation and the horse, Comanche, which belonged to one of the officers of Custer's command.

Just before the battle took place, Sitting Bull left camp and retired to a hill some miles away to "make medicine." He later returned

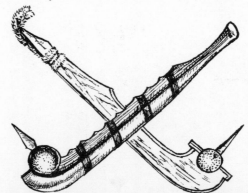

and told the Indians the soldiers were coming and it was he who was responsible for the strategy that led to victory. He did not take part in the fight but continued to make medicine while the battle was in progress and after the fight was over took full credit for the victory.

After Custer's defeat, the Government made a determined effort to capture Sitting Bull and those Sioux still with him. In October, after several meetings under a flag of truce between the Indians and soldiers which failed, a battle occurred and several thousand Sioux warriors surrendered. Sitting Bull and about 400 refused to do so and escaped across the boundary into Canada.

Between 1876 and 1881, Sitting Bull and his followers, now numbering several thousand, lived in Canada under the jurisdiction of the British government. Many attempts were made by the United States to get him to agree to come back to the States. This he would not do but as many of his band had surrendered earlier in July, later he and the Indians still with him came into Fort Buford and gave themselves up. All were then sent to the Standing Rock Agency in North Dakota.

It was now thought that the trouble with Sitting Bull was over, but between the years 1881 and 1890, he became a famous personality. Then in 1890, the Indian Messiah Craze and Ghost Dance broke out among the Sioux of the Standing Rock Agency. At once Sitting Bull saw this as an opportune time to regain his former prestige. He worked upon the Indians telling them that he had seen the Messiah and urging them to revolt. Trouble now broke out once again as the Indians were led to believe that soon their old way of life, their hunting grounds, and the buffalo would be restored to them.

It was evident to the authorities that the Indians would soon get out of hand unless something was done. Sitting Bull was asked to

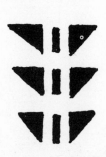

come to the Agency but refused to do so. His arrest was ordered and on December 15, 1890, a detachment of cavalry troops and Indian police were despatched to bring him in. Early that same morning, ten Indian police came into the clearing where the house of Sitting Bull was located and entered to place him under arrest. He agreed to go without trouble, but the Indians living with him tried a rescue and in the fight that followed, Sitting Bull was killed.

Many accounts have been written about how this famous Indian met his death; possibly the truth will never be known. He was buried in the Indian cemetery at the Standing Rock Agency, a true American with his thoughts always for the good of his people.

Geronimo
1834-1909
Apache

CHAPTER IX

Geronimo

1834? — 1909

ABOUT 1834, at the headwaters of the Gila River near old Fort Tulerosa, New Mexico, there was born an Indian who was to become another famous person of early history. This part of the great southwest was wild, arid and mountainous and this Indian boy, born into the Chiricahua Apache tribe, one of the fiercest of all the Indian tribes, was little more than a savage. He was to become known later in life as Geronimo, or Goyathlay, meaning "One Who Yawns."

Due to his cunning and leadership, Geronimo was admitted to the council of braves by the wise men of the tribe at a very early age for an Apache youth. In later years, he became a Chief of the southern Chiricahuas upon the death of Cochise, another well-known Apache leader, but most of his early life seems to have become lost to recorded history.

The Apache, along with the Navaho, are the southernmost offshoot of the Athabascan family of North American Indians. They were noted for their ferociousness and their raiding habits and in both early and late accounts one can find references to these acts of cruelty and the raids upon settlers of the southwest.

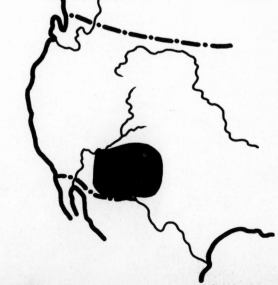

They were divided into two divisions, one found by the Spanish in 1540 living east of the Rio Grande, the other near the headwaters of the Gila River in southern New Mexico and Arizona. In 1903 their total population was about 6,000. Today they are found living chiefly on the Fort Apache Agency and Reservation and the San Carlos Agency and Reservation, both in Arizona. They total approximately 7,000 individuals.

Geronimo's first raids were against the Mexicans as he blamed these people for the murder of his mother, his wife and three small children during his early life. His hatred though of all peoples, other than those of his own tribe, his constant raids, his killing, stealing, and burning, made him one of the most hated and feared Indians of the early southwest. In years to come, Geronimo became known as "Geronimo, the Renegade". He was of a dominating character, possessed of courage, cruelty, intuition and determination, but when one considers his early childhood and the hardships and tortures he was brought up with, it is understood why he was molded into the cruel and ruthless killer he turned out to be.

In 1876, Geronimo requested permission of the authorities to join with other members of the tribe in a move from the Ojo Caliente Agency in New Mexico to the San Carlos reservation in Arizona. His request was granted but as soon as all were off the reservation, the wily Geronimo led them into northern Mexico where they lived for about a year. Now orders were issued by the War Department of the United States Government for his capture, and after a series of military actions, he and his band were captured in New Mexico and taken to the San Carlos Agency in Arizona. Although there were many charges brought against him, including the murder of hundreds

of people, Geronimo was never brought to trial. He was confined to the San Carlos reservation and remained there until 1884 when he again led a small band of Apaches in escape and warfare.

This band of Indians was made up of 42 men, 94 women and children, and from 1884 to 1885, Geronimo led them in a war against the United States which has been called "one of the most remarkable in recorded history." With hardly any food, supplies or ammunition, except what they could get by stealing and capturing from the settlers, they fought against 5,000 regular troops and 500 Indian scouts attached to the United States Army.

Geronimo now led his people into Mexico, but as there was at this time an agreement between the United States and Mexico the troops of both countries joined in hunting them down. The Indians in a series of raids back and forth across the border, killed many ranchers and drove off hundreds of head of stock. Although Geronimo was blamed for these outrages, it has since been proved that his band contained other Indians as cunning, daring and more dangerous than he, and it was these Indians who conducted many of the raids.

After months of being kept on the move by the troops of both countries, Geronimo asked for a truce. In August, 1886, near Skeleton Canyon, Arizona, Geronimo and the remnants of his band, now numbering only 22 warriors surrendered to General Nelson A. Miles. This war, if it may be called that, lasted eighteen months and required pursuit by troops over a distance of 2,000 miles at a cost to the United States Government of more than a million dollars.

After their capture Geronimo and sixteen members of the band, including all the leading Chiefs, were sent to Fort Pickens, Florida, as it was not thought wise to let them remain in the southwest after all the havoc they had caused. Later the entire band of over four hundred Chiricahua Apaches were moved to the Indian Agency at Mount Vernon, Alabama. Then in 1894, Geronimo and another famous Apache Chief, Naiche, were moved to Fort Sill, Oklahoma. There were about 240 people in his band at this time and all were given a reasonable allotment of land and otherwise provided for, but being a people used to a wild and free life, they were never wholly satisfied.

Geronimo had now become known throughout the country. Although he was responsible for the murder of hundreds of people and the cause of millions of dollars being wasted, his presence was in great demand at public affairs. Geronimo attended several expositions notably the World's Fair at St. Louis in 1904. Here he sold photographs and autographs to the curious and made a considerable sum of money. He was not only a brave and cunning Indian when on the warpath, but a shrewd business man in money transactions.

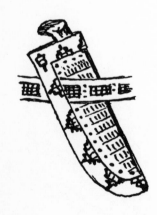

On March 4th, 1905, Geronimo along with five noted Chiefs of other tribes, the Sioux, Comanche, Ute, Blackfoot and his own Apaches, rode in the parade during the inauguration of Theodore Roosevelt as President. Geronimo, at this time and using his popularity to gain admission, appealed in person to President Roosevelt for a pardon. He asked that he and his people be allowed to leave the reservation and return to the old familiar hunting grounds of their ancestors in Arizona, but his request was refused by the President.

Geronimo was returned to Fort Sill and lived there the remainder of his life on the land allotted to him. He died of pneumonia after an illness of only two days in the hospital at Fort Sill, Oklahoma, on February 17, 1909. At death he was about 75 years of age, of which 22 years had been spent as a prisoner of the United States Government.

Chief Joseph
1840-1904
Nez Perce

CHAPTER X

Chief Joseph

1840 — 1904

CHIEF JOSEPH was the last great Chief of the Nez Perce Indians. He was born in the Wallowa Valley of Oregon in 1840, the son of Old Joseph, also a Chief of the Nez Perces. The name Joseph was a family name given them by a missionary. His Indian name in translation means "Thunder Coming from the Water up over the Land."

The Nez Perce Indians were also known as the Chopunnish Indians, and some accounts name them the Nimapu, or Shahaptian. They were the principal group of the confederation, also the largest and easternmost members of the Shahaptian group and the one most affected by living in close contact with the Plains Indians such as the Sioux.

In 1805 the estimated population of this tribe was about 6,000 persons which had dropped to 2,100 in 1921. As they never were a large tribe in numbers there are today possibly as few as 1,000 living on the Nez Perce Reservation in Idaho with a few others, not over a hundred or so, on the Colville Reservation in the state of Washington.

Joseph's early years were spent in a missionary school, a much different beginning in life than many Chiefs of other Indian tribes as his

father, Old Joseph, early in life was converted to Christianity. He was an unusual Indian in many ways, and had always been friendly with the whites. In 1871, Old Joseph died and the leadership of the tribe was now in the hands of his son, Chief Joseph.

Chief Joseph was sometimes called the "Red Napoleon" because of his knowledge of military strategy. He followed a steadfast policy of peace with the whites although treaty after treaty was broken, as he always recognized the great military superiority of the whites and realized that if there was a war, all would be lost to the Indians.

The Nez Perces—the name means "pierced noses," although very few of these Indians practised this custom—lived in the northwestern part of Idaho, and Oregon and Washington. They were first discovered by Lewis and Clark in 1805. In 1855, a large part of their original territory was taken over by the United States Government and the tribe was confined to a reservation which included the Wallowa Valley in Oregon and a large part of Idaho. Some years later, gold was discovered on the reservation and the Nez Perces were ordered to a new reservation near Lapwai, Idaho. The Nez Perce tribe at this time was made up of two distinct bands, the Upper Nez Perces and the Lower Nez Perces. It was this Lower Band, led by

Old Joseph, who refused to leave their homes and this brought about the Nez Perce War of 1877.

In 1871 when Joseph, the son, became Chief, he followed the wishes of his father and refused to order his people from their homes on the reservation. Joseph was a loyal and wise man, and even though he had been taught the ways and desires of the white man and their methods of taking what they wanted when it came to lands owned by Indians, he still refused to leave and to move to another reservation. In the years that followed, many whites flocked into the country and the Indians were treated to all kinds of injustices and humiliation. Even then Chief Joseph held a firm hand and would allow no act of war or harm to the whites by his braves. It was a hard time for Chief Joseph as many of the warriors wanted to declare war on the settlers for the sufferings inflicted upon them.

Nearly all the settlers living in the territory hated the Indians and wanted them moved off the reservation and by force, if necessary. These people wanted the lands belonging to the Indians and they did not want, nor did they intend to pay for the land. Some of these people though who had been friendly to the Indians now stood up for their cause, as they did not want to see the Indians robbed of their homes.

A council meeting at Lapawai, Oregon, was arranged in November, 1876, to see what could be done and Chief Joseph was elected to speak for all tribes that would not sign the new treaty.

Joseph told the whites that "the Indians would not give up their homes. They would not move to a new reservation and start all over again. The Wallowa Valley was their home, it had always been their home, and even though the whites say they will pay for the land the promise would not be kept. Other treaties made had not been kept. The Nez Perces wanted to live as free people, to come and go as they wished, to live now as they had always lived in the past."

General O. O. Howard and another Army officer, both members of the Commission that met with the Indians, stated in their report that since the Government had not lived up to its agreement of the 1855 treaty, the Indians were no longer bound by it. Despite this report, the Commission recommended that Chief Joseph and his band of the Lower Nez Perces be moved to the Lapawi Reservation.

General Howard was ordered to see that the Indians left their homes for the new reservation. Several conferences were held as General Howard wanted the Nez Perces to go of their own free will and to move without trouble or blood-shed. Chief Joseph again at

first refused to go, but later changed his mind and agreed to the move after seeing it was hopeless to resist. Later the warriors of the tribe rebelled and even though Joseph tried to persuade them to move, they decided in council to fight.

The Nez Perces now bought guns and ammunition whenever and wherever they could and began training in military maneuvers. They became a well trained group of Indians and many observers said they were as well trained and as good horsemen as the regular cavalry troops. Warfare was declared and several severe defeats were inflicted on the Government troops under General Howard.

After several months of fighting which took place over a very large area, with sometimes the outcome in favor of the Indians, other times in favor of the troops, Chief Joseph and his band were forced to flee. He conducted a masterly retreat of more than 1,000 miles across the Bitter Root Mountains into Montana. Joseph was trying to reach Canada, but when within a few miles of the border he was surrounded and he and his entire band captured.

The group, now numbering less than 450 individuals, were first taken to Fort Leavenworth, Kansas, and later to the Indian Territory of Oklahoma. In 1883, a small part of women and children were al-

lowed to return to their former homes in the Wallawa Valley and during the following year they were joined by over a hundred others.

Chief Joseph, the leaders of the tribe and those that took an active part in the Nez Perce War, now numbering about 150, were never permitted to return to their valley but were sent to the Colville Reservation in Washington State. Joseph later visited President Theodore Roosevelt in Washington in 1903, pleading to be allowed to return to the land of his people, but this was denied him and he never saw his valley again.

In later years Joseph became reconciled to his fate and to the ways of civilization. He helped in the education of the children of the tribe and used his influence whenever possible to combat the "white man's curse on the Indian," gambling and drink. He died at Nespelim on the Colville Reservation, September 21, 1904.

Quanah Parker
1845-1911
Comanche

CHAPTER XI

Quanah Parker

1845? — 1911

ONE OF THE FEW half-breed Indian Chiefs was Quanah Parker of the Comanches. He was born about 1845 on the Upper Canadian River in Texas. His Comanche Indian name was Kwaina, which means in translation "Fragrant." As a half-breed he used both his Indian name Quanah, and the maiden name of his mother Parker, who was a white woman.

The Comanche were Plains Indians and one of the most powerful and ferocious of all the North American Indian tribes. When first discovered by the French they were living in eastern Colorado and probably numbered about 25,000 at their highest estimate.

The Comanche are credited with being the first of the Indian tribes to obtain horses. These they got from the Spaniards who had brought them over to America. They soon became excellent horsemen in both riding and the breeding of these horses and handled their mounts with remarkable skill in battle. Many accounts are recorded of their horsemanship and daring in warfare. In later years the Comanche family measured its wealth by the number of horses owned by it and horses were sometimes used as a medium of exchange.

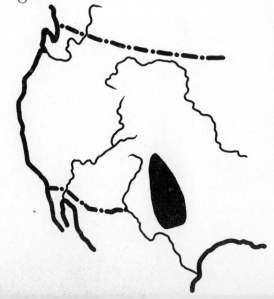

Shortly after their discovery they were pushed southward by the Sioux and were found roving the plains of northwestern Texas. They were at constant war, both against the Spaniards and the other Indian tribes they came into contact with. In these battles they often came out the victor as they were well trained in war-fare and were superior in numbers and owned numerous horses to move quickly.

In the years that followed the opening of the territory hunted over by the Comanches to the settlers, they were the main obstacle for these settlers to over-come and most all the Indian massacres of the southwest during this period could be blamed on the Comanche.

At one time they were forcefully moved to a reservation in Texas but later they ran away. In 1868 most of the tribe again agreed to go on a reservation in western Oklahoma and today they number about 2,500 persons living on the Kiowa Agency and Reservation in that state.

The mother of Quanah Parker was Cynthia Anne Parker who was captured by the Comanches when a small girl. She was brought up by the tribe as an Indian, and only her light blue eyes told that she was of the white and not the red race. When Cynthia Anne grew into womanhood, she married one of the young War-Chiefs of the tribe whose name was Nokoni. Several children were born of this marriage, one of whom was Quanah Parker.

In December, 1860, General L. S. Ross, later Governor Ross of

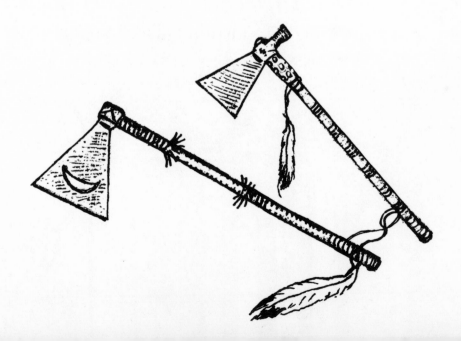

Texas, while leading a detachment of Texas troops, came upon the Comanche village where Nokoni lived with his family. In the fighting that followed, Nokoni was killed and Cynthia Anne Parker and three of her children were captured and brought back to the Army post. One of these three children was Quanah Parker. Cynthia Anne spent the remaining years of her life among her own people after being a captive of the Comanches for twenty-five years.

At the time of his mother's death in 1864, Quanah Parker was about nineteen years of age. Although the son of a Chief he was now an orphan, poor and living among white settlers. He soon was allowed to return to his tribe, but without a family found it lonesome and at times hard to get food. Quanah Parker was an outstanding young man; he knew the ways of the Indian; was a good hunter, intelligent and made friends with both young and old, and soon he was a favorite of the tribe. Later in life and after reaching manhood, although a half-breed, he had all the outward appearances of an Indian. He was tall, straight and dark of skin; in fact he always passed as a full-blood brother of the Comanches and not one who had white blood in him.

Quanah grew up with the tribe and because of his unusual ability even though alone in the world arose to a high position among his people. In 1867, the band of Comanches of which Quanah was now a Chief refused to sign the Medicine Lodge treaty. This treaty would

have sent them to a reservation along with other bands of the Comanches and the Indian tribes of the Kiowa, Apache, Cheyenne and Arapaho. Now the Indians under Quanah and in opposition to the treaty committed acts of war and conducted raids against the settlers, and stealing their horses and cattle. In June, 1874, war was declared between the settlers and the Indians and Quanah was voted by the other Chiefs as the head War-Chief in complete charge. This war continued for nearly a year until troops under the command of General Mackenzie fought the Indians so hard they soon surrendered.

Although conditions were somewhat unsettled, Quanah tried to live the life of an Indian upon a reservation. Even though a half-breed with the ways of the white man in his blood, he found it hard to give up the free life of the Comanche. He had always liked the thrill of war and the raids upon the settlers' stock and particularly his own freedom. Now that his people had surrendered he made the best of new conditions and because of his parentage he was able to adjust to a new way of life much better than some of the other Chiefs and people of the tribe.

As polygamy was customary among the Comanches, Quanah had several wives and a number of children. He was a devoted family man in later years and all his children upon reaching school age had the advantage of a formal education. Later in life several of his daughters married white settlers.

Quanah Parker was considered one of the most influential leaders among the confederated tribes of the Kiowa, Apache and Comanche. In 1882, he proposed leasing of all surplus lands of the reservation to the settlers for grazing their stock. After the agreement was signed and in force, it was found the yearly income from this agreement was over $100,000.00 in cash to the tribe. In 1888, he was appointed to a judgeship in the Indian Court in Texas and was one of the principal signers of the treaty that opened a part of the land of the reservation to the settlers. This was in 1901 and was considered an outstanding accomplishment as very few Indians would ever consent to either leasing or selling reservation land to the settlers.

He was a personal friend of President Theodore Roosevelt and was one of the six Chiefs taking part in the inaugural parade in Washington in March, 1905. The other Chiefs were Little Plume of the Blackfoot tribe; American Horse and Hollow Horn Bear of the Sioux; Geronimo of the Apache; and Buckskin Charley of the Utes. He hunted in later years with the President and called upon him at the White House when in Washington.

Besides his visits to Washington, Quanah Parker travelled to other parts of the country to gain knowledge of the white man and their way of life. In later years he popularized education among the tribe, encouraged the building of permanent houses and helped in making agriculture understood by the Indians. He fought against the Indians

love of drink and was responsible for overcoming such vices among his people. He was so well-known in Texas and nearby states for his good work that a small town in northern Texas was named Quanah in his honor.

In later years, he moved with his family to Oklahoma, near Fort Sill, and built a large and comfortable house known among his people as the "White House of the Comanches." He controlled thousands of acres of lands for the Indians, managing this land and the large herds of cattle and Indian ponies owned by them. Quanah Parker was not only a famous Indian Chief, but a shrewd business man in his dealings with the settlers and the Government. He died in 1911 in his home surrounded by his wives and children.